To my darling daughter

Sofía, I love you more than words can say, but I'm going to try anyway!
You are such an incredible girl! You can do anything you set your mind to. Never
stop reaching for your dreams, because even if you stumble along the way, I will
be there to pick you up and cheer you on!

Your biggest fan,
with so much love,
Mama

BRAVE
STRONG SOFÍA
slays her dragon

'Sofía! Are you up? The movers are outside!'

Sofía wanted to stay in bed, where it was safe and she could hide.

'You don't want to leave what you know behind, but think of the things you're still yet to find. Adventures through towns and streets we don't know… wherever you want, is where we will go.'

Sofía was filled with gloom, as she looked around her empty room.

Rainbows and butterflies that once graced her walls were stuffed in a box being pushed down the hall.

She took a deep breath and put her feet on the ground…

'I can do this.' She whispered. 'Fear won't hold me down.'

Fear was a feeling Sofía felt a lot. Sometimes she'd wake up with her tummy in a knot. She couldn't quite explain exactly what was wrong, she just had a nasty feeling that was really, really strong. It stopped her from doing what she wanted to do; playing with friends and going to school.

'What's wrong, Sofía?' Mama would ask.

'I feel nervous, I want this to pass.'

Her Mama tried to help make the feeling go away, but no matter what she did, the feeling seemed to stay.

The day they moved was just the same... Sofía woke up and the feeling came. It made her want to stay in bed and when she stood up, she was filled with dread. She felt as empty as her bedroom wall as the driver's took everything, curtains and all.

It felt like her safe space was being torn down, as they drove out of her favourite little seaside town.

'Don't worry Sofía, this change will be good. I wish I could take your anxiety, if it was possible I would.'

They were on the road for hours on end, over big hills and around dangerous bends. Sofía reminisced about good times with her friends… hanging out in the park on the weekends.

They drove through a little old town, with a railway and bridge
that were run into the ground.
They passed cities and forests and beautiful countryside; land just
as wild as a ferocious tide.

Sofía thought about why she was nervous to move. It wasn't the people or places she would lose. She chose not to leave her safe space behind, but carry it with her in the back of her mind.

She remembered what her Nanny once said;
'You may feel comfortable tucked up in bed, but the safest places are here in your head. You may not believe me but that's the truth, everything you need to feel OK is inside you.'

They arrived at the house late in the night.
'Come on in Sofía, everything will be alright.'

The door was blue and the windows were tall, it looked nothing like her old house at all.

She took a deep breath and walked inside, found her new room and started to cry.

'Goodnight, Mama, sweet dreams, sleep tight.' Sofía got very little sleep that night.

The morning came and Sofía was stuck. She felt over-whelmed and couldn't get up.

She started to stress when she couldn't take a breath,
she began to sweat and felt heaviness in her chest.
Her Mama came in and knew something was wrong;
'You're going to be OK, Sofía. This won't last too long. Try not to force
a deep breath again, it will come naturally and this feeling will end.'
Her Mama was right... after a minute the deep breath came and her
chest wasn't tight.
She felt a little lighter and her head much brighter.
All it took was a soothing word, a sign to say 'You are seen and heard.'
'Thank you, Mama. I feel much better.'
'You're not alone, we're in this together.'

Sofía was tired of fear and worry, so she dug out her teddy to help in a hurry. If she had another anxiety attack, he'd always be there to have her back.

Sofía was afraid of all things new. Sometimes when it got too much, she didn't know what to do.

New house, new school, new scenery and scents.

'What if I don't fit in or make friends?'

Her Mama taught her some tools to cope...
to replace fear with positivity and hope.
'Anxiety can feel like a bottomless pit, but I promise it will pass.
You just have to believe it! When negative thoughts arise,
welcome them and say; just like a cloud, you too will drift away.'

Sofía tried things she'd never done before. Breathing exercises, positive thinking and more.

She listened to music, swayed in her seat. It helped her to groove to the rhythm and beat. She even learned the 5-4-3-2-1 technique.

This worked well when she felt too scared to speak.

'Find one thing you can taste, two things you can smell, three things you can hear... are they far or near? Four things you can touch and five things you can see. But most importantly, be gentle with yourself, this isn't always easy.'

One thing seemed to help the best, 'slaying the dragon', the unwelcome guest.

She imagined anxiety as the big strong beast and challenged herself to slay it, when it came looking for a feast.

It was hard, she cried, but still she tried. She proved to herself she was stronger than the dragon and never needed to hide.

Sofía had always been a brave little girl, but now she felt ready to take on the world.

Any time anxiety hit, she was equipped with the knowledge and tools to deal with it.

She realised nothing was as bad as it seemed, her new school was fun and her friends were a dream!

Sofía didn't let anxiety stop her anymore. She felt the fear and did it anyway; she was brave to the core.

She repeated a sentence when she felt worry rising:
'This feeling is just a moment in time. It does not control me.
My mind is mine.'